Drones

By Simon Rose

www.av2books.com

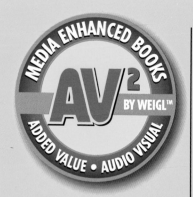

AV² provides enriched content that supplements and complements this book. Weigl's AV² books strive to create inspired learning and engage young minds in a total learning experience.

Your AV² Media Enhanced books come alive with...

Audio
Listen to sections of the book read aloud.

Video
Watch informative video clips.

Embedded Weblinks
Gain additional information for research.

Try This!
Complete activities and hands-on experiments.

Key Words
Study vocabulary, and complete a matching word activity.

Quizzes
Test your knowledge.

Slide Show
View images and captions, and prepare a presentation.

... and much, much more!

Go to www.av2books.com, and enter this book's unique code.

BOOK CODE

H418474

AV² by Weigl brings you media enhanced books that support active learning.

Download the AV² catalog at www.av2books.com/catalog

AV² Online Navigation on page 48

Published by AV² by Weigl
350 5th Avenue, 59th Floor
New York, NY 10118

Websites: www.av2books.com   www.weigl.com

Library of Congress Control Number: 2014940097

ISBN 978-1-4896-2226-6 (hardcover)
ISBN 978-1-4896-2227-3 (softcover)
ISBN 978-1-4896-2228-0 (single-user eBook)
ISBN 978-1-4896-2229-7 (multi-user eBook)

Printed in the United States of America in North Mankato, Minnesota
1 2 3 4 5 6 7 8 9 0   18 17 16 15 14

052014
WEP090514

Weigl acknowledges Getty Images as its primary image supplier for this title.

Project Coordinator: Aaron Carr
Art Director: Terry Paulhus

Drones

CONTENTS

Introduction to Drones

Drones are aircraft that are operated by **remote control** without a human pilot. Also called unmanned aerial vehicles, or UAVs, they can carry sophisticated equipment such as **sensors**, cameras, and weapons. The U.S. military has used drones during the **war on terror** in some countries, including Afghanistan, Iraq, Pakistan, and Yemen. Government officials are interested in using drones for **law enforcement** and border patrols as well. In the future, drones may be used for many **commercial** and personal purposes.

Drones and the Military

"Many different types of drones are now armed and are used in war."

Drones and the Government

"Unmanned aircraft can track people suspected of serious crimes."

Commercial Drones

"Farmers, delivery services, and oil companies are just some of the groups that could use drones."

Personal and Environmental Drones

"An increase in the number of personal drones will probably lead to regulations regarding air traffic and privacy."

Drones and the Military

KEY CONCEPTS

R emote controlled unmanned aircraft were first developed during World War I (1914–1918), when they were used for target practice by pilots. They were also used mostly for the same purpose in World War II (1939–1945). During that war, Germany developed and used an unmanned flying bomb, known as the V-1. After World War II, pilotless aircraft were often used for military **surveillance**. Today, a number of different types of UAVs are still used for surveillance, but many are now armed and are used in war.

1 Military Use of Drones

The role of drones in the U.S. military changed after the terrorist attacks on the United States on September 11, 2001, and the U.S. invasions of Afghanistan and Iraq that followed. Unmanned aircraft became much more important to combat operations. The U.S. armed forces used fewer than 200 military drones in 2002, but more than 11,000 have been used since that time.

Drones have been fitted with more sophisticated equipment and advanced technology, and they have been armed with powerful missiles. They are well suited for the war on terror, in which enemy forces are not usually on a battlefield where ground troops and military aircraft can fight them. The enemy, instead, often hides in remote regions and is hard to find.

Drones can fly for longer than aircraft with pilots and can cover a wider area.

Their equipment can locate the enemy and attack targets on the ground, without putting a pilot in danger. The drone is either flying on its own or is being controlled by an operator who could be thousands of miles away. Drones can be very accurate in finding their targets, but sometimes **civilian casualties** do occur.

> "The United States and about 50 other countries now use military drones."

Some military experts believe that one day, remotely operated drones could replace most types of manned military aircraft. Small drones are also being developed, and some can be launched by being thrown from a soldier's hand. These drones could help ground forces to safely observe enemy troops at close range.

The United States and about 50 other countries now use military drones. The U.S. military's drones are manufactured by U.S. companies. Some countries, including Israel, China, and Iran, also build their own versions.

Small drones are mainly used by the military to gather information about possible targets and other areas of interest.

2 Features of Military Drones

One of the leading benefits of drones is that a pilot or **flight crew** is not needed. If drones are damaged or shot down during a mission, they can sometimes be recovered. If they are lost, at least human pilots are not killed, wounded, or captured.

Drones are sometimes more effective in battle than traditional aircraft because they can do things that manned planes cannot. G-force is the force that gravity exerts on an object. G-forces increase during rapid **acceleration**. Pilots often experience this, and people can be injured if g-forces go above a certain level. Since drones have no pilot, g-forces are not a concern. Drones can move more quickly if they need to avoid enemy fire.

Pilots are able to fly for a limited amount of time before they get tired and need to return to base. This limits the length of a mission, which could cause important information on the ground to be missed. Even though the operator at the base may need to be changed, the drone itself can stay in the air. This means that there will be a better chance of a target being located.

Space is not needed in drones for a pilot, **life-support systems**, or safety devices. As a result, drones can maneuver, or move about, better than manned aircraft. They can also hover, or hang in the air without moving, for longer periods at a lower **altitude**.

Hovering allows drones to gather information more effectively. They can also be made in very small sizes. Drones can be sent on missions where they observe the enemy without being seen.

Should Drones Be Used as a Weapon of War, Even if No Official State of War Exists?

Drones are often used by the United States to target terror suspects in countries with which the United States is not officially at war. The U.S. government does not always ask permission from the countries before launching drone attacks. The targets are often wanted in many countries for organizing crimes, but they are not traditional **combatants** in a military situation.

Military Commanders

The war against terror is not like a conventional war, where specific rules need to be followed. Unconventional methods, such as drone attacks, are needed to conduct war against terrorists.

U.S. Government Officials

We need to be careful in selecting targets for drone attacks, but terror suspects may be legitimate targets if they are known to have committed crimes. Sometimes, drones are the only means by which these people can be punished.

Some Political Leaders

There should be more cooperation with the governments of countries where terror suspects are based. It is important to stop new terrorist attacks, but the rights of other countries should be respected.

Human Rights Activists

Even in an unconventional conflict such as the war on terror, governments should follow the established international rules of war. Using drones to kill terror suspects who have not been put on trial and convicted is murder.

For | Supportive | Undecided | Unsupportive | Against

3 Drone Technology

In the U.S. military's MQ-1 Predator drone, electronic controls are located where the **cockpit** would be in a manned aircraft. Navigation systems provide information about the drone's location. The person on the ground remotely operating the drone can communicate with other personnel by using high-frequency radio signals.

Below the cockpit area is the turret. In the **reconnaissance** version of the Predator, the turret area has advanced monitoring equipment. This includes video and **infrared** cameras that can tilt and rotate, as well as **radar**.

The Hunter/Killer version of the Predator is armed with two Hellfire missiles. The drone has an infrared **laser** designator to help find targets.

Sensors calculate targeting information. The Predator can then fire its own missiles, or it can transmit data to ground forces or airborne pilots so that they can destroy the target.

For a simple reconnaissance mission, a Predator can be programmed to operate on its own. For a more complicated mission, it can be directed from the ground by pilots and sensor operators. Drones have onboard computers that monitor many systems.

Another drone, the MQ-9 Reaper, can also be equipped with a combination of surveillance equipment and weapons. This depends on its mission. The Reaper can carry four Hellfire missiles and two laser-guided bombs.

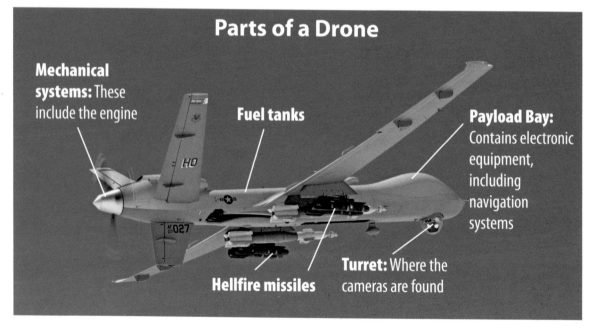

Parts of a Drone

Mechanical systems: These include the engine

Fuel tanks

Payload Bay: Contains electronic equipment, including navigation systems

Hellfire missiles

Turret: Where the cameras are found

⁴ Types of Military Drones

The MQ-1 Predator first flew in 1994. The aircraft has a **wingspan** of 48.7 feet (14.8 meters) and is 27 feet (8.2 m) long. The Predator has a top speed of 135 miles per hour (217 kilometers per hour) and can reach an altitude of 25,000 feet (7,620 m). The Predator has a large fuel tank and can stay in the air for 24 hours.

The MQ-9 Reaper is based on the Predator but is more advanced. It has a wingspan of 65.9 feet (20.1 m) and is 36.1 feet (11 m) long. The Reaper has a top speed of 300 miles per hour (485 km per hour), can fly at 50,000 feet (15,240 m), and can stay in the air for up to 27 hours. The Reaper can carry both missiles and bombs. It can be used to locate and destroy enemy troops and vehicles on the ground.

The RQ-4 Global Hawk is one of the U.S. military's largest UAVs. It is 44 feet (13.4 m) long and has a wingspan of 116 feet (35 m). The Global Hawk can reach speeds of 400 miles per hour (644 km per hour) and can stay in the air for 36 hours. It can operate at an altitude of 60,000 feet (18,300 m). The Global Hawk is used for long-range missions to gather **intelligence**, as well as for general surveillance. In 2001, the Global Hawk became the first unmanned aircraft to fly across the Pacific Ocean, traveling from California to Australia.

An example of a small drone is the RQ-14A Dragon Eye, which weighs only 5 pounds (2.3 kilograms) and has a wingspan of just 45 inches (114 centimeters). The Dragon Eye, which is used for surveillance, can transmit, or send, video images of areas it flies over. The drone can be launched by hand or with a bungee cord, and it has a very quiet motor. The remote-control equipment is small and light enough to be carried in a backpack.

The Dragon Eye drone, which is carried in a backpack in sections, can be assembled in 10 minutes.

5 Accuracy of Drones

Although civilian deaths often occur in war, planned **air strikes** against enemy targets, involving different types of aircraft, do not usually cause civilian casualties. In recent conflicts, most of these casualties have happened when ground troops are attacked and then call in air strikes, sometimes in densely populated areas. Bombs or gunfire rather than drones usually cause civilian casualties in these cases.

According to most statistics, drones are less deadly to civilians than other weapons, such as bombs, machine guns, or **mines**. Drones can locate targets in remote areas and fire missiles with great accuracy. Despite this, sometimes mistakes are made and innocent men, women, and children are hurt or killed. Civilian casualties may occur when a drone misses its target. At other times, an error may have been made in selecting the target.

There are also effects on the drone operator, even if there are no civilian deaths. Following a mission, pilots and soldiers usually stay on a base close to where the fighting happened. They have time to think about their actions before they return home. Drones, in contrast, are often operated remotely by people who are thousands of miles from the battlefield. Drone operators often do not have much of a break between their military and civilian lives. They can go home to their families after a day at work that may have involved causing the deaths of people.

If drone operators made mistakes that led to civilian deaths, they may suffer from emotional problems. These may be so severe that the drone operators can no longer be able to do their jobs. Operating a drone may seem like a video game, but it can sometimes be deadly for innocent people halfway around the world.

U.S. drone strikes against suspected terrorists in Pakistan have led to protests by people in that country.

Should Governments Be Held Responsible for Civilian Deaths Resulting from Military Drone Strikes?

Military drones are often used by the U.S. government to target terrorists. Civilians have been killed in Afghanistan, Pakistan, and Yemen by rockets fired from drones. Such deaths also occur in other parts of the world where drones are used by the military. Some people believe that the governments responsible for such deaths should face criminal charges. Others think that civilian casualties are a result of war that cannot be avoided.

Human Rights Activists

A full independent legal investigation should be conducted into the results of drone strikes. The deaths of civilians are unacceptable, and those responsible should be held accountable.

International Legal Specialists

When drone strikes cause civilian casualties, governments should give money to the families of victims. They should also provide financial assistance to help to repair damage.

U.S. Department of Defense Officials

Efforts should be made to ensure that civilian casualties are kept to a minimum when drone strikes are authorized. However, as in any conflict, some civilian casualties may turn out to be unavoidable.

Military Commanders

In all warfare, civilian casualties are sometimes inevitable. Governments should not face criminal charges if such casualties result from drone strikes that target terror suspects.

| For | Supportive | Undecided | Unsupportive | Against |

Drones and the Government

Customs and Border Protection

HOMELAND SECURITY

KEY CONCEPTS

1 Border Patrols

2 Police Surveillance

3 Search and Rescue Missions and Disaster Relief

4 Firefighting and Forest Fire Detection

5 Weather Forecasting and Research

Although many people think of drones as military devices, other government agencies are also interested in using them. Drones can be used for border protection and surveillance, especially in remote areas. Some law enforcement agencies plan to use them to fight crime. Drones have already been put to work in weather forecasting, and they could be used as well for firefighting and for search and rescue operations.

1 Border Patrols

U.S. Customs and Border Protection (CBP) is part of the Department of Homeland Security. The CBP's Office of Air and Marine operates unarmed Predator drones at the country's borders with Mexico and Canada. The drones, based in Arizona and North Dakota, fly on law enforcement and homeland security missions. In addition, a version of the drone called the Guardian, which is for use over water, operates from bases in Florida and Texas. These aircraft fly over the Caribbean Sea and the Gulf of Mexico.

The northern and southwestern borders of the United States, with Canada and Mexico, are more than 7,000 miles (11,265 km) long. Large parts of these borders run through remote or difficult terrain. These areas are not easy for people to patrol in vehicles, and large numbers of patrol staff would be required. Drones can be used to watch the country's borders 24 hours per day and seven days a week. Drones can detect **smugglers**, terrorists, and **undocumented immigrants**. Data collected by the drones' cameras and sensors can be transmitted to control centers on the ground. Border protection officials can then decide on the best course of action.

The CBP has carried out surveillance to gather information for other government agencies, including the Federal Bureau of Investigation, the Coast Guard, and Immigration and Customs Enforcement. Countries in Europe, the Middle East, and other parts of Asia are studying the use of unmanned aircraft to patrol their land and sea borders.

Border patrol drones fly an average of seven to nine hours on each mission, providing information to agents on the ground.

2 Police Surveillance

Law enforcement agencies can use drones in a number of different ways. Unmanned aircraft can track people suspected of serious crimes. They can also be used to help police manage crowd control and detect traffic violations.

In addition, drones can be used for regular surveillance of entire cities. This provides the police with video and photographic data that can be analyzed after crimes occur in a particular area. Criminals could be observed committing crimes, as well as making their escape. This makes the job of the police much easier. Using unmanned aircraft can mean that fewer officers would be needed to patrol a city. This would save money for the police department.

Drones have advantages over helicopters. They can hover over areas for long periods. They can remain undetected, especially if they are small, while helicopters are very visible. Drones are also less expensive to buy and operate than helicopters.

Police departments have to apply to the U.S. Federal Aviation Administration (FAA) for permits to fly drones. There are safety concerns about adding more aircraft to crowded airspace in cities and towns. There are also privacy concerns. Surveillance by police drones can help to prevent or solve crime and to protect the public. Some people, however, are worried about how drones that take pictures of citizens going about their daily lives will affect personal privacy.

Having an accurate estimate of crowd numbers is useful if there are safety issues or emergencies.

Does the Use of Drones for Surveillance Violate Privacy Rights of Citizens?

L aw enforcement and security agencies are very interested in using drones to help them do their jobs more effectively. Drones patrolling a city or town allow police to watch for crimes that may be taking place and locate the criminals. However, some people believe that drones invade personal privacy and should be restricted.

Privacy Advocates
There are already too many cases of governments spying on their own citizens. Drones should not be used by domestic law enforcement agencies for surveillance under any circumstances. People who are not suspected of a crime should not be watched and photographed by the police.

Supporters of Civil Liberties
Law enforcement agencies should be able to use drones to protect the public. However, privacy must be respected, and independent examiners should have full access to all police procedures.

Local Government Officials
There should be some controls on the use of drones. However, too many restrictions on police use of this technology would hurt law enforcement operations. It is important to protect the public from crime.

Law Enforcement Officials
Effective law enforcement surveillance by all means possible is crucial to preventing many different types of crime today. If people have not committed any crimes, they have nothing to worry about if they are photographed.

| For | Supportive | Undecided | Unsupportive | Against |

3 Search and Rescue Missions and Disaster Relief

Drones have recently provided help following hurricanes, floods, and other natural disasters. They were used, for example, after Hurricane Sandy struck the eastern United States in 2012. They were also used the next year following Typhoon Haiyan in the Philippines.

Drones were used as well when a tsunami, or large sea wave, hit Japan's Fukushima nuclear power plant in March 2011, after an earthquake had occurred. Unmanned aircraft were able to inspect the damaged nuclear reactors. If human crews had done the inspections, they might have been exposed to dangerous **radiation**.

After natural disasters, aid workers need to find out very quickly how much damage has occurred, how many people might be affected, and where the people are who most need help. Streets and roads might be blocked, which could make it difficult to determine the extent of the damage. However, drones can be sent to the area very easily. They can then gather information so that rescue teams and aid workers can make plans quickly and efficiently. Drones can mean the difference between life and death for disaster victims on the ground.

Drones with still, video, and infrared cameras can fly for long periods over a wide area. They can help to find missing people. A drone equipped with **thermal imaging** technology can identify survivors under rubble.

Unmanned aircraft can also help to keep search and rescue teams safe. After a disaster, there might be broken gas lines, spilled fuel, and other hazards, as well as looters. Drones can quickly provide information about conditions in disaster zones, so that relief workers can do their jobs safely. Drones can also be used to deliver urgent medical supplies to remote areas or places that are difficult to reach quickly.

Large drones were used to get aerial views of the damaged Fukushima nuclear power plant from a high altitude.

4 Firefighting and Forest Fire Detection

Fighting forest fires is another area where drones can be useful. In the western United States, wildfires have become more frequent in recent years. Forests, homes, and other buildings have been destroyed. In some cases, firefighters have lost their lives.

Drones can patrol forests that are in high-risk areas for wildfires. If a fire breaks out, they can alert firefighters and monitor the area. Forest fires can spread very quickly. Unmanned aircraft can be equipped with computers and **global positioning systems** (GPS). These can provide firefighters with up-to-date information on a fire's size and location. Firefighters can keep track of changing weather conditions and predict the likely path of the flames. Then, they can decide on a plan to deal with the fire. They can also make a decision on whether people living in the area need to evacuate, or leave their homes.

Drones can fly through smoke much better than manned aircraft, because of their sensors. A pilot's view from the cockpit might be obscured, but drones can use infrared cameras to see through thick smoke. Drones can also stay in the area for longer periods of time and can fly more

In firefighting, drones are often less expensive to operate than helicopters, as well as more effective.

safely and easily at night. In addition, a drone can act as a receiver and transmitter for cellular signals when cell phone towers are not close by. This is very important in remote areas, helping firefighters to stay in touch with each other and with their base.

For safety reasons, current FAA regulations allow the U.S. Forest Service to operate a drone only if it is always in sight of a manned aircraft. This reduces the effectiveness of the drone because its range and time in the air are limited to those of the other aircraft. If these rules were changed, firefighters might be able to use drones more often in their operations.

5 Weather Forecasting and Research

Drones are proving to be very useful for weather forecasting and research, especially for studying hurricanes, other tropical storms, and tornadoes. Manned flights have been launched to collect data on severe weather in the past. Drones can do this without putting pilots and crews at risk.

A small drone called the Tempest has been used to investigate supercell thunderstorms, which are the type of thunderstorms that produce tornados. The drone's flights were part of a research project into how tornados are formed. The Tempest is only 10 feet (3 m) wide and weighs 20 pounds (9 kg), with a top speed of around 100 miles per hour (160 km per hour). Its instruments can measure wind speed, air pressure, moisture, and temperature. The data then can be transmitted to a ground tracking station.

The National Aeronautics and Space Administration (NASA) has a program for studying tropical storms, using large Global Hawk drones. These UAVs can fly much higher and for longer than manned aircraft. Weather satellites can observe storms from space, but the Global Hawk can get much closer. It can take still pictures and video, measure weather conditions, and gather detailed information about the storm. Scientists hope to learn why some tropical storms do not last very long before fading away, while others develop into deadly hurricanes. NASA's Global Hawks have flown over storms in the Atlantic and Pacific Oceans as well as in the Gulf of Mexico.

Organizations Using Drones in the United States, 2012

The FAA has given a number of organizations permission to operate drones in U.S. airspace. Different types of users account for varying percentages of all drone traffic.

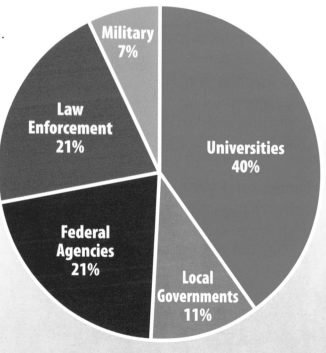

Military 7%
Law Enforcement 21%
Universities 40%
Federal Agencies 21%
Local Governments 11%

Should the Use of Drones Be Limited Because They May Be Captured by Criminals?

There are concerns about the use of UAVs for illegal activity. For example, smugglers could use drones to cross borders. Drones are very expensive to purchase. However, criminals might try to steal government-owned drones. Some people believe that security measures can prevent criminals from capturing and using drones. Others feel that the threat of drones being captured is real and, therefore, the use of UAVs should be restricted.

Campaigners for Public Safety
There is a definite possibility that drones could be captured and used against the police or security services. This makes them too much of a risk to be employed to protect the public.

Technology Experts
It might be difficult for criminals to capture drones, but any security system can be overcome, given the right level of expertise. This makes the theft of drones a real danger.

Government Scientists
Even if a drone could be captured, it is unlikely that criminals would have the knowledge to operate such a high-technology aircraft. They would also not be able to bypass security controls to use the drone.

Security Officials
Security procedures are already in place that will stop any attempt to capture a drone. No government drones could ever be used or adapted by criminal groups.

| For | Supportive | Undecided | Unsupportive | Against |

Commercial Drones

KEY CONCEPTS

1 Surveying and Agriculture

2 Home and Office Delivery

3 Pipeline and Power Line Inspections

4 Photography and Archaeology

5 The Media and Private Security Companies

The FAA currently restricts flights by drones in U.S. airspace. Other countries have similar rules. However, this is likely to change in the future, and a number of possible commercial uses for drones have been proposed. The U.S. Congress passed a law in 2012 telling the FAA to come up with safety standards and other new rules for drone flights. The goal is to have UAVs flying in U.S. airspace by 2015, along with manned aircraft. In late 2013, the FAA named six government agencies and universities to test civilian versions of drones, as a step toward developing safety rules.

1 Surveying and Agriculture

Companies involved in searching for natural resources can use drones to explore Earth's surface. **Geologists** observe rock formations in remote areas from above, to help determine what might be below the surface, such as supplies of oil and gas. Drones can do this faster and more efficiently than other types of surveys. Using drones, rock formations can be scanned at low altitude with laser and infrared sensors to investigate possible energy resources. Computer software can also create three-dimensional, or 3D, maps from thousands of **digital** images captured by drone cameras.

Agriculture is another area where drones can be used. In some parts of the world, including the United States, farms are often very large. Farmers have to travel long distances by car or truck to check on crops and livestock. By using drones for this, farmers save time and money, and they use less fuel to drive around their property.

The drones can take pictures of fields or even individual plants to check their growth patterns. Farmers can then determine where water or fertilizers might be most needed. Farmers can also use drones to spray **pesticides**, fertilizers, and other chemicals on their fields. In some countries, such as Japan, small drones are already used to spray crops on steep hillsides that cannot be reached easily with tractors.

Some American farmers are already using drones. The FAA currently limits flights above 400 feet (150 m) by unmanned aircraft in the United States. However, flights to spray crops or survey distant fields and monitor herds of livestock are usually below this altitude. In addition, most large American farms and ranches are in rural areas. Drones in these places are less likely to interfere with other **air traffic**.

2 Home and Office Delivery

In late 2013, the large online **retailer** Amazon.com announced plans for an aerial home delivery service for its products. Small, unmanned aircraft would be used to deliver packages weighing about 5 pounds (2.2 kg) or less. These packages account for more than 80 percent of the company's business. The company predicted that products could be delivered to a person's home within 30 minutes of being purchased on Amazon's website, provided that the person lived near an Amazon warehouse. It would likely be several years before Amazon carried out its plan.

The delivery services UPS and DHL are also studying the use of drones for deliveries. In Australia, a company that sells textbooks announced plans to work with a drone company to send books to customers. The U.S. Postal Service and government-run mail services in other countries deliver billions of packages every year. If drones become common in the skies, government mail services are likely to be using them too.

Commercial drones would be able to carry only lighter items, so human delivery services will still be needed. Drone delivery services would most likely be used only in cities and larger towns and not in rural areas, at least at first. This is because there would be more business in densely populated areas.

In the future, commercial drones could transform many aspects of daily life. Cell phones and other mobile devices mean that people do not need to be at a home address to receive a delivery. They could order products, using their cell phones, to be delivered to their office or other location. Even pizza could be delivered by drone. Research is also being carried out to develop large unmanned drones to transport cargo over long distances.

Even if drone delivery becomes common, it is likely that large and heavy products will still have to be delivered by truck.

Should Commercial Drones Be Limited Because of the Possible Effect on Existing Delivery Services?

I f restrictions on commercial drones are eased in the United States and other countries, there will likely be many more remote-controlled small aircraft in the skies. Some people think that this will lead to the end of the current mail system and private delivery services. Others do not believe this is likely to occur.

Business Analysts
The postal service is already under threat from online communication, such as email. Drones and similar devices will make the situation harder for postal and messenger services. These services will become outdated, and many people will lose their jobs.

Economists
Aerial delivery would provide more competition for government mail and private delivery services. They will need to look for ways to make deliveries faster and at lower cost. If they can, people will benefit. However, if they cannot, current delivery services may not survive.

Technology Experts
Aerial delivery vehicles would likely be very costly to operate. This means they will take some business away from current delivery services, but probably not enough to cause these services to go out of business.

Safety Experts
Drones are not practical for delivering packages to homes or offices. It may be unsafe to have large numbers of drones traveling around busy cities. UAVs will not be able to replace today's delivery services.

For   Supportive   Undecided   Unsupportive   Against

3 Pipeline and Power Line Inspections

Oil and gas companies have large facilities, both on land and offshore, which can be difficult to monitor. Drones can make this job easier. They can, for example, inspect parts of an offshore **oil platform** that are hard to see or are risky for workers to reach. Drones can check for leaks or other safety problems, helping to prevent accidents. If a disaster occurs at an oil platform, the workers are forced to leave, but the energy company still needs to know what is happening there. Small drones can observe the situation at close range and more safely than helicopters and other manned aircraft.

Planes and helicopters already make hundreds of flights every day to offshore oil platforms, such as those in the Gulf of Mexico. Flying drones in areas with heavy air traffic raises safety concerns. However, energy companies are hopeful that these problems can be solved.

Oil and gas companies have **pipelines** that often run for hundreds of miles through remote areas or in harsh terrain such as deserts. Unmanned aircraft with cameras can provide regular surveillance of pipelines. They can check for leaks or other problems at a much lower cost than helicopters or planes with crews.

Utility companies, which provide services such as electricity, natural gas, and water, can also use drones. Overhead power lines can be damaged during storms. Winter conditions, blocked roads, or fallen trees can prevent utility companies from sending in workers to assess the situation. Drones can inspect power lines and send details on any damage. Then, if there is an outage, power can more quickly be restored.

Iraq has bought drones from the United States to help protect its oil platforms.

4 Photography and Archaeology

Hollywood filmmakers have used aerial cameras for many years to shoot scenes for movies. Helicopters have usually been used for this, but drones with cameras attached offer more options at lower cost. Some real estate agents are using drones to shoot video tours or take aerial photos of homes for sale.

Drone photography could become a major business in the future. Festival organizers can take still pictures and videos of their events from the sky. Not only does this capture the scene, but it also estimates crowd numbers. Wedding photographers can use drones to hover and provide special views of the ceremony. In the future, drones the size of baseballs could be used to provide guided tours of museums or historic sites.

Uses also exist in the field of **archaeology**. Before an excavation, or dig, can begin, archaeologists create maps of an area, which involves detailed work on the ground. Sometimes, there are also aerial surveys done using planes and balloons. Mapping on the ground and in the air using these methods can take months or even years, but drones can often do this in days or weeks.

Drones have been used at excavation sites in Peru to capture images to create 3D maps. In Peru, many archeological sites are under threat from human development. Areas have to be surveyed quickly to see if they contain valuable artifacts before construction work destroys the sites. Drones produce the needed maps much more quickly than is possible with traditional methods.

Archaeologists in other countries have also used drones. In Belize, an aerial survey by drones helped archaeologists to locate ancient structures that they had failed to find after years of work on the ground.

According to the FAA, a person can operate a remote-controlled aircraft with a camera and shoot video for personal use.

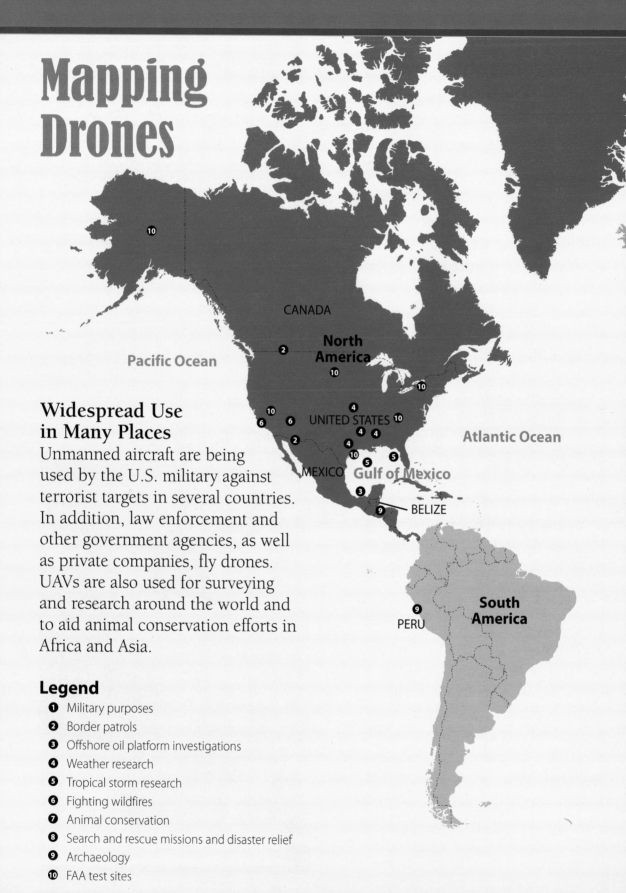

Mapping Drones

CANADA

North America

Pacific Ocean

UNITED STATES

Atlantic Ocean

MEXICO **Gulf of Mexico**

BELIZE

South America

PERU

Widespread Use in Many Places

Unmanned aircraft are being used by the U.S. military against terrorist targets in several countries. In addition, law enforcement and other government agencies, as well as private companies, fly drones. UAVs are also used for surveying and research around the world and to aid animal conservation efforts in Africa and Asia.

Legend

❶ Military purposes
❷ Border patrols
❸ Offshore oil platform investigations
❹ Weather research
❺ Tropical storm research
❻ Fighting wildfires
❼ Animal conservation
❽ Search and rescue missions and disaster relief
❾ Archaeology
❿ FAA test sites

Arctic Ocean

Asia

Europe

JAPAN
8

IRAQ
1

AFGHANISTAN
1

NEPAL
7

PAKISTAN
1

LIBYA
1

Pacific Ocean

YEMEN
1

Africa

1 SOMALIA

PHILIPPINES
8

MALAYSIA
7

INDONESIA
7

Indian Ocean

Australia

SOUTH AFRICA
7

Southern Ocean

SCALE

1,200 Miles

1,200 Kilometers

5 The Media and Private Security Companies

So far, drones have not been used a great deal by journalists, but this may soon change. Small remote-controlled aircraft that can fit into a backpack might become standard equipment for reporters. The drone's cameras could take photographs and videos that would be impossible or too dangerous for journalists to take with hand-held cameras.

Celebrities are often in the news, and reporters and photographers regularly follow their activities. Drones could fly over celebrities' homes or other places where they expect to have privacy. While laws are already in place in many countries to protect privacy, the rules about gathering news or taking photographs with drones are not very clear. If unmanned aircraft are going to be used by the media, new regulations may be needed.

Cameras attached to drones are also useful for private security companies. These companies monitor businesses and private homes, providing protection from break-ins and other criminal activity. Drones would provide security surveillance from the air as well as from ground level. They would therefore allow security companies to offer better service.

The use of drones by security companies also raises questions about privacy. The cameras attached to a drone might take pictures of other houses or of people on the street. Some countries and U.S. states have laws against photographing private property. These types of laws may be difficult to enforce if drones become common.

Drones and Air Traffic

The world's busiest airports are in major cities where drones are likely to be more common in the coming years.

Hartfield-Jackson, Atlanta, Georgia (USA) 95,462,867

Beijing Capital, Beijing (China) 81,929,359

London Heathrow, London (United Kingdom) 70,037,417

Tokyo International, Tokyo (Japan) 66,795,178

Chicago O'Hare, Chicago, Illinois (USA) 66,633,503

Los Angeles International, Los Angeles, California (USA) 63,688,121

Charles de Gaulle, Paris (France) 61,611,934

Dallas/Fort Worth, Dallas, Texas (USA) 58,591,842

Soekarno-Hatta, Jakarta (Indonesia) 57,772,762

Dubai International, Dubai (United Arab Emirates) 57,684,550

Figures are for numbers of passengers in 2012

Will Privately Operated Drones Be a Hazard to Air Traffic, Especially in Large Cities?

Air traffic from commercial aircraft is very heavy above the largest cities around the world. Experienced personnel are capable of handling commercial drone traffic. However, large numbers of privately operated drones, owned by individuals rather than companies, will increase the volume of air traffic over highly populated areas.

Air Traffic Controllers
Air traffic problems already occur in many of the world's major cities. With many drones in the sky, traffic would be much harder to regulate. There would be a major risk of collisions involving UAVs.

Airspace Regulators
Privately operated drones would need to be heavily regulated to protect the public. The people who operate drones would need to be trained and tested. Otherwise, there could be many air accidents.

Market Analysts
Drones will fly lower than commercial aircraft over densely populated areas. This will limit the dangers regarding the number of aircraft in the air at any one time.

Operators of Private Drones
Air traffic is already at high levels over the world's major cities, and it is very well regulated. More privately operated drones will not cause problems.

| For | Supportive | Undecided | Unsupportive | Against |

Personal and Environmental Drones

KEY CONCEPTS

Unmanned aircraft are an option for protecting the environment and for monitoring **endangered** animals in remote locations. In addition, radio-controlled aircraft for personal use have been available for decades. Technological advances have changed these "hobby" drones in significant ways.

1 Personal Drones

Basic types of radio-controlled aircraft are operated using a joystick located on a device called a controller. This device uses radio waves to send instructions to the plane. The person on the ground controlling the aircraft is always in sight of it.

Today, more sophisticated models can be equipped with a camera, and some people believe that this makes the planes drones. Today's small aircraft can also be controlled with special goggles. Using these, the operator can be inside a building. He or she just needs an antenna outside the building that is in range of the aircraft. The goggles allow the person to see whatever the camera is viewing. Some remote-controlled aircraft also have GPS. They can then be sent miles away from where the operator is based.

These aircraft can fly over backyards and peer into windows. Businesses can use them to spy on competitors. Small hobby drones raise questions about privacy and trespassing. In the United States, the FAA is considering new regulations about their use.

2 Monitoring the Environment

Researchers are using drones to study the effects of **climate change** in Antarctica and Greenland. Images and data collected by drones help scientists. The drones can collect information from remote areas that would not be easy to reach otherwise.

Drones can inspect remote coastlines, coral reefs, and offshore animal refuges, looking for signs of environmental damage. They can also look for illegal activity. For example, they can be used to catch polluters who are disposing of hazardous materials at sea or in rivers and lakes.

In some European countries, drones are used to inspect large forests to see if the trees show any signs of disease. Sometimes, many trees have to be cut down to try to stop an outbreak of a disease or an attack of pests. Drones can help find problems before they become serious. Forest managers can then take action to avoid losing a large number of trees. They can also observe wildlife **migration patterns** and the movement of animals to different feeding grounds.

3 Protecting Endangered Animals

Endangered **species** are at risk for a number of reasons, including climate change, loss of habitat, and **deforestation**. However, rhinos, elephants, and tigers are mostly in danger from poachers. These people hunt animals illegally and sell the horns, tusks, or other body parts.

The killing of African elephants by poachers has doubled since 2008. It is difficult for government forces to patrol large game reserves, or land set aside for animals, and protect animals from poachers. Drones can help them to monitor these areas.

The World Wildlife Fund (WWF) is helping governments in Africa in their efforts against poachers. In 2012, the WWF received a $5 million grant from Google to help develop drones to protect endangered animals. The drones carry different types of cameras, including some for night vision or thermal imaging. The drone operator uses a laptop computer to view what the drone sees with its camera. Then, park rangers on the ground can be notified if poachers are spotted. The rangers can try to catch the poachers before they hurt the animals.

The Orangutan Conservancy uses aerial surveys by drones to study orangutans in Malaysia and Indonesia. This is much easier than doing surveys on the ground in the thick tropical forests where orangutans live. Another organization using drones is Sea Shepherd. The group uses drones to monitor whaling ships to determine if laws protecting whale populations are being broken.

Rhinos in Danger

Along with African elephants, rhinos in Africa are among the species most at risk from poachers. The number of poachers caught each year has increased a great deal since 2010. However, in spite of efforts to arrest poachers, the number of rhinos killed has gone up as well.

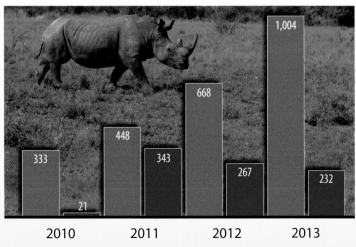

	2010	2011	2012	2013
Rhinos killed	333	448	668	1,004
Poachers arrested	21	343	267	232

- ■ Rhinos killed ■ Poachers arrested

Is It Effective to Use Drones to Protect Endangered Species?

Endangered animals such as elephants and rhinos mostly live on game reserves in remote areas of Africa. Drones can monitor remote areas and help to stop poachers, who kill thousands of animals each year. However, some people believe that drone flights are not effective in protecting endangered animals.

African Governments

Drones can provide constant monitoring of endangered animals in large remote reserves. It is too expensive to hire enough guards to patrol these reserves. However, using information from drones, guards can go where they are needed.

Animal Protection Groups

Even if drones do not stop all poachers, they also help animals in other ways. Drones can monitor the way animals move around in remote areas. This information can help governments create policies on land use and development that will protect animals.

Drone Experts

Unless they are armed and have human operators, drones can only observe endangered animals. They cannot directly protect animals from poachers on the ground. If guards are not nearby, they may not be able to get to the scene of a problem fast enough to catch the poachers.

Some Environmentalists

Many types of animals are endangered for reasons other than poaching, such as destruction of their environment. The use of drones is expensive and does nothing to prevent these problems. The money used for drones could be better spent to protect animals in other ways.

For   Supportive   Undecided   Unsupportive   Against

Drones through History

Since the first pilotless aircraft were developed and tested in World War I, UAVs have become an established part of the U.S. military. They are also now being used for a number of civilian purposes.

1935

The British Royal Navy begins flying the Queen Bee, a returnable and reusable UAV. The Queen Bee is radio-controlled, and this type of drone is used for target practice by military groups until the 1940s.

1941

The U.S. Army Air Corps begins production of the OQ-2 Radioplane as a target drone. The OQ-2 could stay in the air for about one hour.

1944

During World War II, Germany launches the first V-1 "flying bomb" against Great Britain. It carries a 1-ton (0.9-tonne) warhead that explodes on impact. Thousands of V-1s hit London.

1946

1946

Eight B-17 Flying Fortresses are used as remote-controlled drones by the U.S. military. They collect data from radioactive clouds during atomic tests conducted in the Pacific Ocean.

1951

The Ryan Firebee, which can be launched from the ground or from a plane in the air, is introduced. Different versions are used by the U.S. military from the 1950s to the 1970s for reconnaissance missions over North Korea, China, and Southeast Asia.

1979

Israel develops the Scout drone. This UAV, used to gather intelligence, is flown during Israel's 1982 conflict in Lebanon.

1985

1985

Israel introduces the Pioneer drone. Some of these aircraft are bought for use by the U.S. armed forces.

1991

The United States uses Pioneer UAVs against Iraq in the Persian Gulf War.

1994

The MQ-1 Predator completes its first flight for the U.S. military. It enters service the following year.

2001

The RQ-4 Global Hawk makes the first nonstop flight across the Pacific Ocean by an unmanned aircraft. Two years later, the FAA authorizes the Global Hawk as the first UAV to operate in United States airspace.

2002

The RQ-7 Shadow enters service with the U.S. Army. It flies its first mission the following year during the Iraq War.

2007

The MQ-9 Reaper, a larger and improved version of the Predator, flies its first combat mission, in the Afghanistan war.

2012

The WWF receives funding from Google to adopt advanced technology, including drones, to protect endangered animals.

2007

2013

Amazon.com announces that it is testing drones for a home delivery service.

2001

Working with Drones

MILITARY DRONE OPERATOR

Duties Conducts unmanned aircraft missions for reconnaissance, surveillance, and targeting

Education Must pass specific armed services tests and undergo basic combat training, followed by advanced training and on-the-job instruction

Interest Remote-controlled and radio-controlled vehicles, computer systems, and analysis of information

Military drone operators control the flights of UAVs from remote locations. Sometimes, the drones gather intelligence to help military commanders plan operations. At other times, the planes are used to attack the enemy. Drone operators fly large unmanned aircraft, such as the Predator or Reaper, as well as smaller models. Operators are responsible for running all the drone's cameras, sensors, and other instruments.

AERONAUTICAL ENGINEER

Duties Designs different types of aircraft and aircraft **propulsion** systems

Education A bachelor's degree in aerospace engineering and a master's degree in aeronautical engineering

Interest Mathematics and science, including algebra, calculus, physics, chemistry, electronics, aviation, and computer science

Aeronautical engineers help to design aircraft, including UAVs, and their many parts and systems. Engineers work with both civilian and military aircraft, and they may be involved in developing technology such as weapons and radar. Aeronautical engineers assess new aircraft during flight tests. They also work in aircraft maintenance and may be called on to investigate the causes of accidents. Aeronautical engineers may be employed by private companies or government agencies.

SOFTWARE ENGINEER

Duties Designs and develops computer software

Education A bachelor's degree in mathematics, software engineering, computer science, or systems engineering

Interest Science, mathematics, programming, and problem solving

Software engineers design, develop, test, and evaluate computer software. These are the programs that make computers run, allow computers to communicate with other devices, and enable computers and other electronics devices to perform specific tasks. Engineers may design many different types of software, including programs for aircraft operation, military weapons systems, computer games, and business record-keeping. Computer systems software engineers develop and maintain the entire computer system of a large organization. Some software engineers work for private companies, and others are employed by various government agencies.

DATA ANALYST

Duties Analyzes data and presents it so that others can make decisions

Education A bachelor's degree in accounting, business, computer science, mathematics, or statistics

Interest Mathematics, statistics, and data

Data analysts work in a number of different industries. They are responsible for studying statistics and other information, understanding what the data are showing, and summarizing the results of this analysis for others to understand. These other people then use the information to make decisions. In business, the results of data analysis could be used to plan new products or sales campaigns. In the military, data analysts involved with UAVs examine the information collected by drones. They then create a report so that commanders can decide on a course of action.

Key Drone Organizations

DOD

Goal Protecting the national security of the United States

Reach United States and worldwide

Facts Largest employer in the United States, with more than 3.2 million active service men and women, members of the National Guard and Reserves, and civilian workers

The U.S. Department of Defense (DOD) directs the U.S. armed forces and assists the president in protecting the national security of the United States. The DOD's headquarters are at the five-sided office building known as the Pentagon, located near Washington, D.C, in Arlington, Virginia. The Department of Defense includes the U.S. Army, Air Force, and Navy. There are military bases in both the United States and other countries. Personnel work in combat and peacekeeping situations around the world.

FAA

Goal Regulation and oversight of all aspects of U.S. civil aviation

Reach United States

Facts Includes 35,000 employees responsible for managing air traffic in the skies over the United States and at U.S. airports

The Federal Aviation Administration (FAA) is part of the U.S. Department of Transportation. Besides regulating air traffic, the agency is responsible for controlling aircraft noise and the environmental effects of civil aviation. The FAA is also responsible for giving out licenses to pilots, doing flight inspection, research, and development. In late 2013, the FAA announced a program to research the impact of drones on civil aviation in the United States.

EFF

Goal Protecting people's privacy and freedoms in the modern world

Reach Worldwide

Facts One of the world's leading organizations working to make sure that present-day technology is not used in ways that harm people's rights

The Electronic Frontier Foundation (EFF) was founded in 1990 and has its headquarters in San Francisco, California. The organization works on issues involving free speech, personal privacy, and consumer rights. The EFF uses lawyers, activists, and technology specialists to fight cases in the courts, sometimes against large corporations or the U.S. government. The EFF also works to inform the media and the public about policies or situations that it believes threaten people's rights and freedoms in today's world.

WWF

Goal Protecting endangered species and environments around the world

Reach Worldwide

Facts Has more than 5 million supporters in 100 countries

The World Wildlife Fund (WWF) is an international organization founded in 1961. The WWF works to protect endangered species, prevent harm to the environment, and make people aware of the risks posed by deforestation and climate change. The WWF focuses many of its efforts on problems affecting certain animals or involving specific regions around the globe. These problems include rising temperatures in the Arctic, deforestation in the Amazon rain forest, and threats to the survival of African and Asian animals such as rhinos, tigers, and elephants.

Research a Drone Issue

The Issue

Drones are the subject of much debate. Many groups may not agree on the best way to regulate drones. It is important to enter into a discussion to hear all the points of view before making decisions. Discussing issues will ensure that the actions taken are beneficial for all involved.

Get the Facts

Choose an issue (Political, Cultural, Economic, or Ecological) from this book. Then, pick one of the four groups presented in the issue spectrum. Using the book and research in the library or on the Internet, find out more about its point of view. What is important to the group? Why is it backing or opposing the particular issue? What claims or facts can it use to support its point of view? Be sure to write clear and concise supporting arguments for your group. Focus on drones and how the group's needs relate to them. Will this group be affected in a positive or negative way by action taken regarding drones?

Use the Concept Web

A concept web is a useful research tool. Read the information and review the structure in the concept web on the next page. Use the relationships between concepts to help you understand your group's point of view.

Organize Your Research

Sort your information into organized points. Make sure your research clearly answers what impact the issue will have on your chosen group, how that impact will affect it, and why the group has chosen its specific point of view.

DRONE CONCEPT WEB

Use this concept web to understand the network of factors related to drones.

- Used for surveillance and offensive operations
- Civilian casualties may result from drone attacks
- Can be an effective weapon against terrorists in remote regions

- Drones can be used to protect endangered animals from poachers
- UAVs survey glaciers and other areas to track climate change
- Drones can monitor threatened forests, coastlines, and oceans

- Police use drones to prevent and solve crime
- UAV patrols protect international borders
- Drones may help to combat smuggling and illegal immigration

Military Drones

Environmental Protection

Law Enforcement

DRONES

Commercial Drones

Privacy and Legal Issues

Government and Civilian Drones

- Can locate natural resources and monitor pipelines
- Used by filmmakers and the media
- Potential delivery vehicles, but this use faces challenges

- Help with fighting wildfires and protecting firefighters
- Avoid putting humans at risk during storm research
- Can be the difference between life and death after natural disasters

- Drones can be used to spy on people
- Laws regarding privacy may be unclear
- Regulations regarding use of airspace may need to change

Test Your Knowledge

Answer each of the questions below to test your knowledge of drones.

1 What does UAV stand for?

2 What event took place early in the 21st century that changed the role of drones in the U.S. military?

3 What large company provided money to the World Wildlife Fund for using drones to protect endangered animals?

4 How many missiles does a Predator drone carry?

5 What was the first unmanned aircraft to fly across the Pacific Ocean?

6 About how many countries currently use military drones?

7 What is the name of the U.S. government agency that regulates civil aviation?

8 What is the top speed of the MQ-9 Reaper?

9 What can farmers do with drones and chemicals to care for their crops?

10 The U.S. government currently limits flights above what height by unmanned aircraft?

ANSWERS 1. Unmanned aerial vehicle **2.** The attacks of September 11, 2001 **3.** Google **4.** Two **5.** The Global Hawk **6.** 50 **7.** Federal Aviation Administration (FAA) **8.** 300 miles per hour (485 km per hour) **9.** They can spray chemicals on fields from drones **10.** 400 feet (150 m)

Key Words

acceleration: a change in the speed or direction of an object

air strikes: attacks made by aircraft

air traffic: the movement of aircraft within a specific space

altitude: the height of an object such as an aircraft above sea level

archaeology: the study of past human life and culture by examining buildings, graves, pottery, and tools

civilian casualties: people who are not members of armed forces who are injured, killed, captured, or missing as a result of military conflict

climate change: a change in average temperatures and other weather conditions over a long period of time, such as the major warming trend that many scientists agree has been taking place over the past century

cockpit: the part of a plane where the pilot is located

combatants: people engaged in combat or fighting

commercial: related to buying and selling products or services

deforestation: clearing large areas of forest without planting new trees to replace those removed

digital: the method of storing, using, and sending information, sounds, and pictures in the form of numbers, which is used by computers and other electronic devices

endangered: at risk of becoming extinct, or no longer surviving in the world

flight crew: the pilots and other people responsible for operating an aircraft

geologists: people who study the origin, history, and structure of Earth, such as rock formations

global positioning systems: systems that uses signals from satellites to tell locations

infrared: producing or using rays of light that cannot be seen

intelligence: information about the enemy

laser: a device that produces a powerful, narrow beam of light

law enforcement: ensuring obedience to the laws of a country or local area, usually done by the police

life-support systems: equipment that makes it possible for life to survive in conditions that would otherwise be deadly

migration patterns: established movement of people or animals

mines: bombs that are placed in the ground or in the water that explode when they are stepped on or touched

oil platform: a structure used in drilling for oil

pesticides: chemicals that kill insects, weeds, or other living things that harm crops

pipelines: lines of pipe with pumps, valves, and control devices for transporting liquids and gases

propulsion: the force that moves something forward

radar: a method of detecting distant objects by analyzing certain types of radio waves reflected from the objects' surfaces

radiation: waves or particles that give off a form of energy that may be harmful to people and other living things

reconnaissance: the inspection of an area to gather military information

remote control: the control of a machine from a distance by using radio waves to send instructions or coded signals

retailer: a person or company that sells products directly to the individual customers who will use them

sensors: mechanical devices that are sensitive to light, temperature, or radiation levels and transmit signals to another device where they can be evaluated

smugglers: people who take items into or out of a country illegally

species: groups of animals with common characteristics

surveillance: the monitoring of people's activities or information about them, often for security reasons or military purposes

thermal imaging: using the heat given off by an object to produce an image of it or locate the object

undocumented immigrants: people who do not have the required government permission and papers to enter the United States

war on terror: the ongoing campaign by the United States, begun after the attacks of September 11, 2001, to fight international terrorism

wingspan: the distance between the tip of one wing and the tip of the other wing on an aircraft

Index

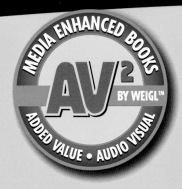

Log on to www.av2books.com

AV[2] by Weigl brings you media enhanced books that support active learning. Go to www.av2books.com, and enter the special code found on page 2 of this book. You will gain access to enriched and enhanced content that supplements and complements this book. Content includes video, audio, weblinks, quizzes, a slide show, and activities.

AV[2] Online Navigation

Audio
Listen to sections the book read alou

Book Pages
AV[2] pages directly correspond to pages in the book.

Video
Watch informative video clips.

Key Words
Study vocabulary, and complete a matching word activity.

Embedded Weblinks
Gain additional information for research.

Try This!
Complete activities and hands-on experiments.

Quizzes
Test your knowledge.

Slide Show
View images and captions, and prepare a presentation.

AV[2] was built to bridge the gap between print and digital. We encourage you to tell us what you like and what you want to see in the future.

Sign up to be an AV[2] Ambassador at www.av2books.com/ambassador.

Due to the dynamic nature of the Internet, some of the URLs and activities provided as part of AV[2] by Weigl may have changed or ceased to exist. AV[2] by Weigl accepts no responsibility for any such changes. All media enhanced books are regularly monitored to update addresses and sites in a timely manner. Contact AV[2] by Weigl at 1-866-649-3445 or av2books@weigl.com with any questions, comments, or feedback.